Extinction Is Forever

by Donald Silver

illustrated by Patricia J. Wynne

Carolina Parakeet, extinct 1914

Julian Ⓜ Messner

Silver Burdett Press • Parsippany, New Jersey

For Bill Jewett
—D.S.

Thanks to Dr. Niles Eldredge of the American Museum of Natural History
for his comments and insights.

JULIAN MESSNER
Published by Silver Burdett Press
299 Jefferson Road, Parsippany, New Jersey 07054
Copyright © 1995 by Donald Silver
Illustrations © 1995 by Patricia J. Wynne
JULIAN MESSNER and colophon are trademarks of Simon &
Schuster.
Manufactured in the United States of America.

10 9 8 7 6 5 4 3 2 1

Library of Congress Cataloging-in-Publication Data

Silver, Donald M.
    Extinction is forever / by Donald Silver ; illustrated by Patricia
J. Wynne.
        p.   cm.
    Includes bibliographical references.
    1. Extinction (Biology)—Juvenile literature. 2. Man—
Influence on nature—Juvenile literature. [1. Extinction
(Biology) 2. Man—Influence on nature.] I. Wynne, Patricia,
ill. II. Title.
QH78.S54 1995 575´.7—dc20 93-32567 CIP AC
ISBN 0-671-86769-5 (hardcover)
ISBN 0-671-86770-9 (paperback)

Giant Horsetail,
extinct 230 mil

Moa, extinct about 1900

Tasmanian Wolf, ex

Great Auk, extinct 1844

Contents

Great Blue Butterfly,
extinct 1979

Introduction

An airplane is about to land on Oahu, one of the Hawaiian Islands in the Pacific Ocean. It is flying east from Guam, an island thousands of miles away. On the ground, police and special agents are ready to search the plane. There may be a hitchhiker on board too dangerous to let into Hawaii.

Even before the plane lands, the agents watch it closely through binoculars. As the plane pulls into the gate, they check the runway. And when the door opens to let passengers off, the agents head instead for the cargo bay and wheels. The hitchhiker they seek isn't human; it is the brown tree snake.

The people of Hawaii have good reason to want to keep out the snake. Over a period of 30 years, this species, or kind, of snake killed most of the forest birds living in Guam. Today, there are thousands of brown tree snakes on Guam. They climb anything they can, from trees to telephone poles to airplane tires.

The Hawaiian Islands have no bird-eating snakes. Birds on these islands may never have even seen such a predator—an animal that wants to eat them. If brown tree snakes reach Hawaii and lay eggs, a lot of birds will die. However, for the honeycreepers and many other kinds of birds the arrival of the snakes could mean the end forever. These species live only on the Hawaiian Islands. If the brown tree snakes wipe them out, there will be none left anywhere else on Earth. They will become extinct.

This book is about extinction. But it is about more than saving birds from snakes. It is the story of a great unsolved mystery: Why did dinosaurs, woolly mammoths, and countless other kinds of living things disappear, never to be seen again?

4

Brown Tree Snake

Micronesian Kingfisher

5

Digging Up the Past

No human being has ever seen a dinosaur alive. Yet everyone knows that Apatosaurus had a long neck and a small head, that Triceratops grew three horns, and that Tyrannosaurus was a fierce meat eater with sharp teeth and deadly claws.

The last dinosaurs became extinct about 65 million years ago, long before humans appeared on Earth. That being the case, how do we know that they even existed? How do we know enough to create dinosaur halls in museums, books about dinosaurs, or scary dinosaur movies?

We know about the dinosaurs because they left behind bones, teeth, footprints, and egg shells. As centuries upon centuries passed, these became fossils. A fossil is anything that remains of an animal or plant that lived a long time ago. You'll read more about fossils and how they often turned to stone on page 44.

Most fossils are found in rocks that form very slowly in layers. Different layers contain different kinds of fossils. After carefully digging fossils out of rock layers and studying them, scientists called paleontologists can figure out the age of the rock layers and the fossils within them.

The first dinosaur fossils show up in rock layers about 230 million years old. Fossils of other kinds of animals such as sharks and snails are also found in rock layers 230 million years old and in rocks older than that. This tells scientists that there were sharks and snails living on Earth before there were dinosaurs as well as when the first dinosaurs appeared.

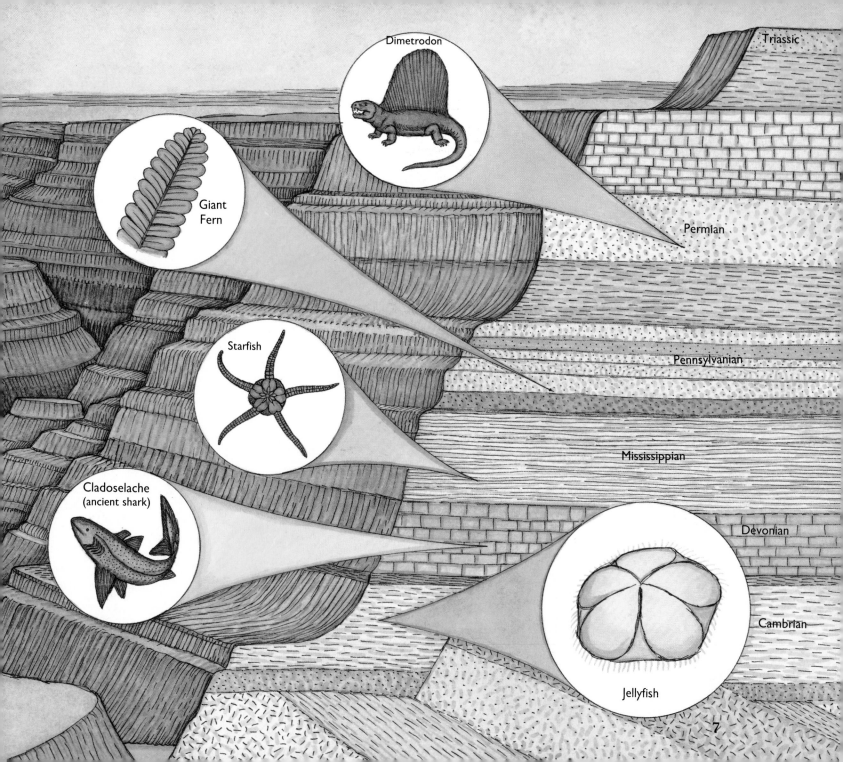

Triassic

Permian

Pennsylvanian

Mississippian

Devonian

Cambrian

Dimetrodon

Giant Fern

Starfish

Cladoselache
(ancient shark)

Jellyfish

7

Plesiosaur

pterodactyl

Icthyosaur

8

Vanishing Fossils

Everything we know about dinosaurs comes from fossils. Fossil teeth reveal if a dinosaur ate plants or other animals. Fossil skulls show the size of each dinosaur brain. With complete skeletons to study, scientists can tell where the dinosaur's muscles were located and how they moved.

Dinosaur fossils have been discovered in rock layers that are between 230 and 65 million years old. After 65 million years ago, they vanish. Not one dinosaur fossil has ever been found in rocks that formed between 65 million years ago and today. The absence of dinosaur fossils from this time period means an extinction took place.

Dinosaur fossils weren't the only fossils to vanish 65 million years ago, however. Fossils of flying reptiles called pterodactyls and of swimming reptiles called plesiosaurs and ichthyosaurs also disappeared. These creatures became extinct along with the dinosaurs. So did many other kinds of living things, but not all.

Fossils of fishes, crocodiles, turtles, birds, and small mammals are found in rock layers formed before the dinosaurs died out, when the dinosaurs died out, and after the dinosaurs died out.

Unanswered Questions

Why did crocodiles survive but not dinosaurs? Why weren't all birds wiped out along with all pterodactyls? Why didn't shark fossils disappear with those of plesiosaurs and ichthyosaurs? What saved small mammals from becoming extinct? So far, few facts about what happened 65 million years ago are known for sure. Paleontologists can study the same fossils and come up with different ideas about what caused extinction. What do you think wiped out the dinosaurs?

9

Back to the Past

Imagine traveling back in time 65 million years. Your mission is to find out what really happened to the dinosaurs. *You are there:* What evidence are you looking for?

Is a mysterious creature devouring all dinosaur eggs until none are left? Then there will be no young dinosaurs to take the place of the adults when they die. That would mean extinction.

Or is some deadly disease killing off the dinosaurs? If that's the case, then look for sick pterosaurs, plesiosaurs, and ichthyosaurs. What about crocodiles and mammals? They might not be as sick as the dinosaurs. One day they might recover.

10

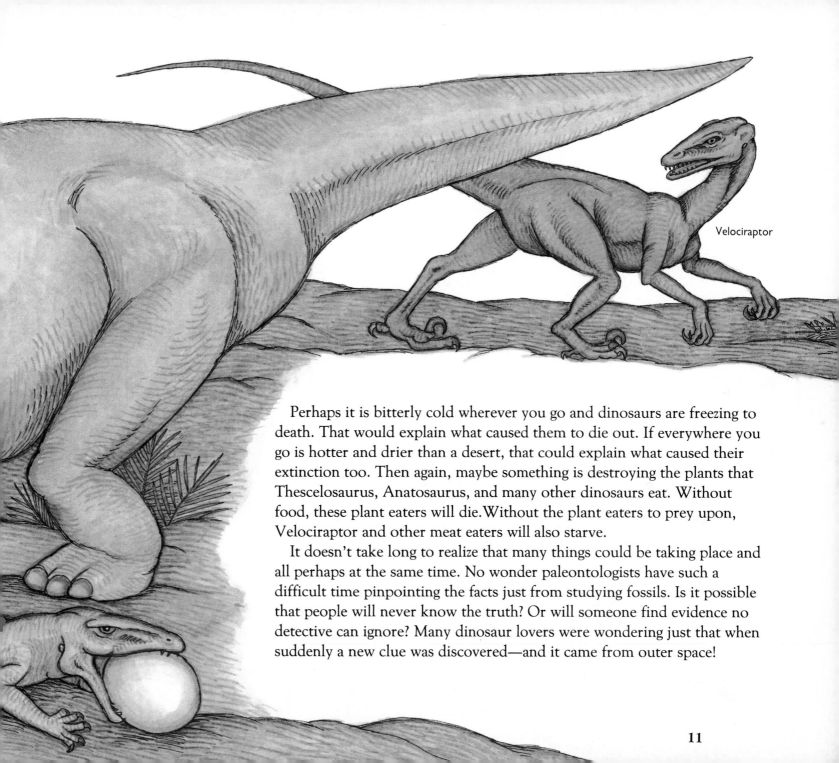

Velociraptor

Perhaps it is bitterly cold wherever you go and dinosaurs are freezing to death. That would explain what caused them to die out. If everywhere you go is hotter and drier than a desert, that could explain what caused their extinction too. Then again, maybe something is destroying the plants that Thescelosaurus, Anatosaurus, and many other dinosaurs eat. Without food, these plant eaters will die. Without the plant eaters to prey upon, Velociraptor and other meat eaters will also starve.

It doesn't take long to realize that many things could be taking place and all perhaps at the same time. No wonder paleontologists have such a difficult time pinpointing the facts just from studying fossils. Is it possible that people will never know the truth? Or will someone find evidence no detective can ignore? Many dinosaur lovers were wondering just that when suddenly a new clue was discovered—and it came from outer space!

The Death Rock

In the late 1970s, a group of scientists made an exciting discovery. While studying a layer of rock near Gubbio, Italy, they found the metal called iridium. The scientists knew at once that they had discovered something unusual because there is very little iridium in most Earth rocks. More importantly, the iridium-rich layer was about 65 million years old.

Was there some connection between iridium and what happened to the dinosaurs? The scientists thought so. They pointed out that iridium is found in rocks whirling through space. These rocks, called asteroids and meteoroids, sometimes crash into Earth. If such a rock crashed into our

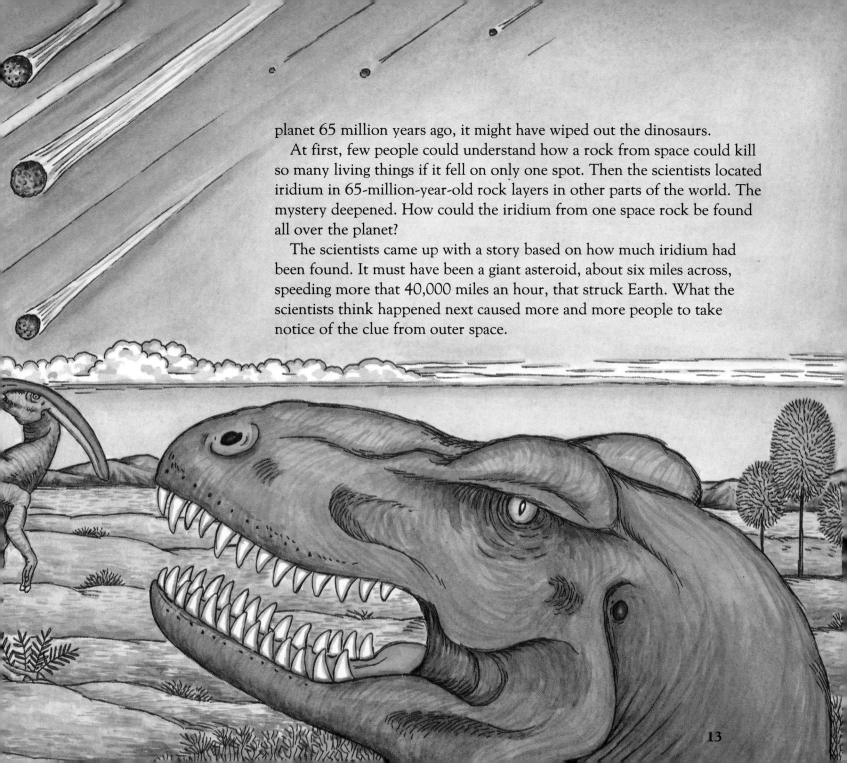

planet 65 million years ago, it might have wiped out the dinosaurs.

At first, few people could understand how a rock from space could kill so many living things if it fell on only one spot. Then the scientists located iridium in 65-million-year-old rock layers in other parts of the world. The mystery deepened. How could the iridium from one space rock be found all over the planet?

The scientists came up with a story based on how much iridium had been found. It must have been a giant asteroid, about six miles across, speeding more that 40,000 miles an hour, that struck Earth. What the scientists think happened next caused more and more people to take notice of the clue from outer space.

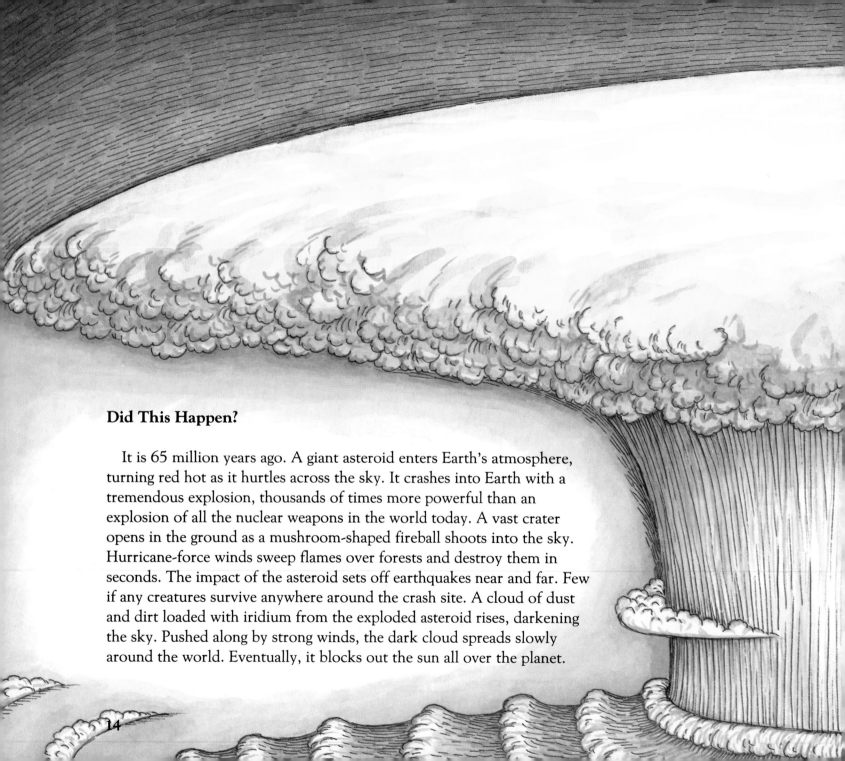

Did This Happen?

It is 65 million years ago. A giant asteroid enters Earth's atmosphere, turning red hot as it hurtles across the sky. It crashes into Earth with a tremendous explosion, thousands of times more powerful than an explosion of all the nuclear weapons in the world today. A vast crater opens in the ground as a mushroom-shaped fireball shoots into the sky. Hurricane-force winds sweep flames over forests and destroy them in seconds. The impact of the asteroid sets off earthquakes near and far. Few if any creatures survive anywhere around the crash site. A cloud of dust and dirt loaded with iridium from the exploded asteroid rises, darkening the sky. Pushed along by strong winds, the dark cloud spreads slowly around the world. Eventually, it blocks out the sun all over the planet.

For many months, none of the sun's rays reach Earth's surface.

Without solar energy, the temperature on Earth drops and warmer climates become bitter cold. In the now sunless world, plants no longer make food. Land and water plants begin to die. Plant eaters, weakened by the cold, slowly starve to death. Soon meat eaters cannot find anything to eat.

None of the dinosaurs survive the aftermath of the asteroid explosion. Pterosaurs, plesiosaurs, ichthyosaurs, and many other creatures are wiped out too. Animals that live underground and store their food or those that sleep through cold winters manage to survive. So do buried plant seeds and fungi. Little by little, the iridium-rich dust and dirt settle to Earth's surface. They form a thin layer that becomes part of the rock that scientists will discover 65 million years later.

Not So Fast

Not everyone was convinced by the asteroid theory. Other scientists pointed out that there is iridium deep inside the Earth that comes out of erupting volcanoes. Those scientists think that about 65 million years ago hundreds of volcanoes exploded at the same time. Each volcano blasted smoke and ash loaded with iridium into the sky. Winds swept the smoke and ash around the globe blocking out the sun for months.

Poisonous gases shooting out of the volcanoes killed many forms of life and caused deadly acid rain to fall. Floods of lava poured across the land and hardened into rock. That's the same rock you can find in the Deccan region in India today.

Was it the asteroid from outer space or was it the exploding volcanoes that wiped out the dinosaurs? "Both," said yet another group of scientists. They are certain that the dinosaurs died out gradually over millions of years. All the asteroid and the exploding volcanoes did was to hasten what was going to happen anyway.

If it sounds as though the scientists are fighting with each other, they aren't. No one can say for sure what took place 65 million years ago and what it had to do with the end of the dinosaurs. Do you think it matters since the dinosaurs are gone anyway?

# Extinction Is a Part of Nature

The mystery of the missing dinosaurs is just one piece of an even greater puzzle. Dinosaurs weren't the first living things to disappear forever. Nor were they the last.

Long before dinosaurs roamed Earth, there were dunkleosteuses, seymourias, diadecteses, scutosauruses, and thousands of other kinds of animals. They left fossils before the last of their kind died out. Perhaps millions of species that lack fossil remains also became extinct. Many scientists today believe that 99 percent of all the species that ever existed on Earth have died off. What caused them to become extinct is still unknown.

The mystery of extinction is as great as the mystery of life itself. Finding out what causes extinction matters for several reasons. One reason is because humans do not want to follow the dinosaurs into extinction. Another reason is that if there is a way to prevent extinction from happening, we want to know about it. And thirdly, extinction is part of the way nature works—something that people will always be trying to understand.

What happened to the dinosaurs 65 million years ago is called a *mass extinction*. When a mass extinction occurs, a large number of species on land and in the ocean die out at about the same time. Nearly 70 percent of all species living 65 million years ago were wiped out with the dinosaurs. Another type of extinction is called *background extinction*. Only a few species die out over a year, or 10 years, or 50 years, or 100 years. Background extinction goes on all the time. It has been taking place ever since life began.

After the dinosaurs

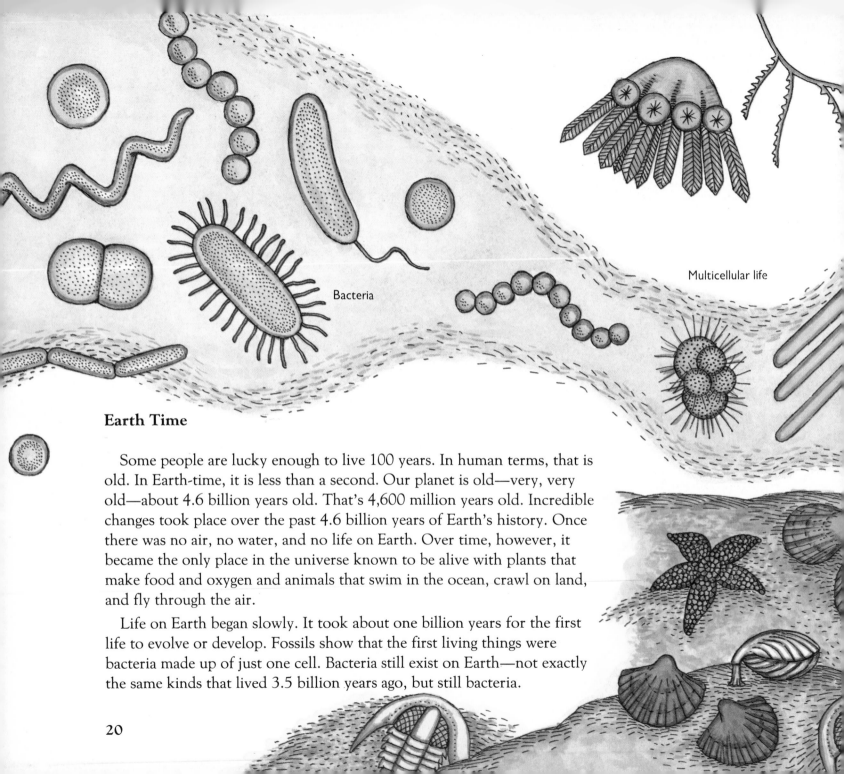

Bacteria

Multicellular life

Earth Time

Some people are lucky enough to live 100 years. In human terms, that is old. In Earth-time, it is less than a second. Our planet is old—very, very old—about 4.6 billion years old. That's 4,600 million years old. Incredible changes took place over the past 4.6 billion years of Earth's history. Once there was no air, no water, and no life on Earth. Over time, however, it became the only place in the universe known to be alive with plants that make food and oxygen and animals that swim in the ocean, crawl on land, and fly through the air.

Life on Earth began slowly. It took about one billion years for the first life to evolve or develop. Fossils show that the first living things were bacteria made up of just one cell. Bacteria still exist on Earth—not exactly the same kinds that lived 3.5 billion years ago, but still bacteria.

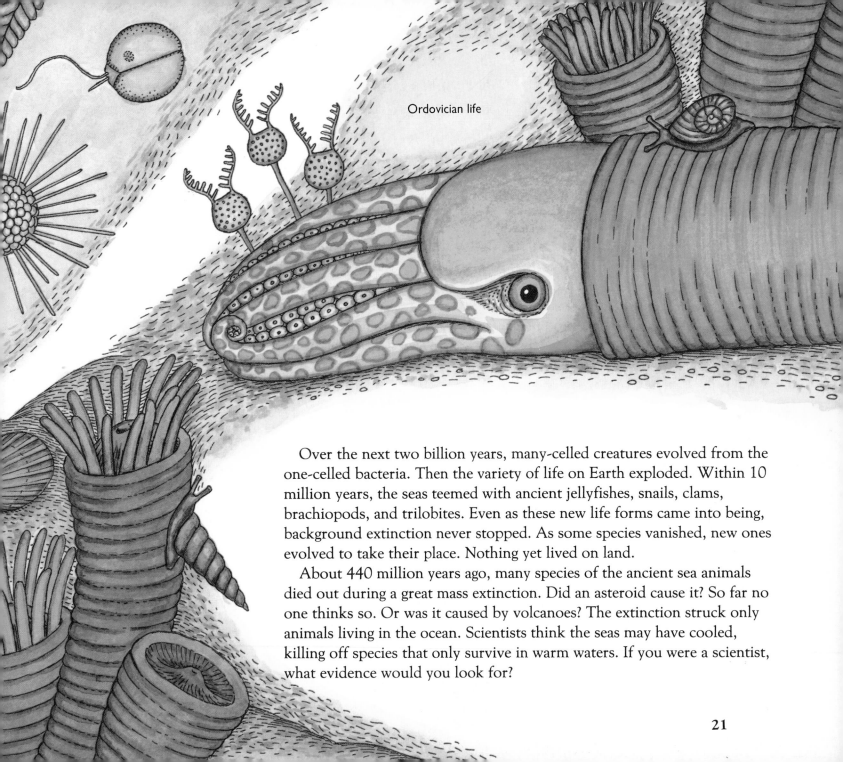

Ordovician life

Over the next two billion years, many-celled creatures evolved from the one-celled bacteria. Then the variety of life on Earth exploded. Within 10 million years, the seas teemed with ancient jellyfishes, snails, clams, brachiopods, and trilobites. Even as these new life forms came into being, background extinction never stopped. As some species vanished, new ones evolved to take their place. Nothing yet lived on land.

About 440 million years ago, many species of the ancient sea animals died out during a great mass extinction. Did an asteroid cause it? So far no one thinks so. Or was it caused by volcanoes? The extinction struck only animals living in the ocean. Scientists think the seas may have cooled, killing off species that only survive in warm waters. If you were a scientist, what evidence would you look for?

21

The Biggest Extinction of All

Earth's biggest extinction took place about 250 million years ago. Almost 96 percent of all species from land and water were wiped out. Imagine how frightening a place Earth would be if nearly every plant, animal, fungus, and one-celled creature alive today stopped existing. That's just what happened 250 million years ago.

Earth looked very different back then. Instead of the separate continents we know in the world today, there was one giant land mass surrounded by one vast ocean. Instead of the flowering plants familiar to us today, there were giant club mosses and horsetails. Instead of frogs and toads, there were Diplocauluses with boomerang-shaped heads and many other giant amphibians. Fierce mammal-like reptiles called therapsids preyed upon plant eaters large and small.

Very little is known about what caused the terrible loss of life or how long it lasted. Once again, there is no sign that an asteroid had anything to do with this extinction. Some scientists think that exploding volcanoes followed by deadly acid rains and frigid temperatures were responsible. No matter what the cause was, life went on and millions of new species continued to evolve. From the reptiles that survived the biggest extinction came dinosaurs and mammals, including the ancestors of human beings.

Earth 250 million years ago

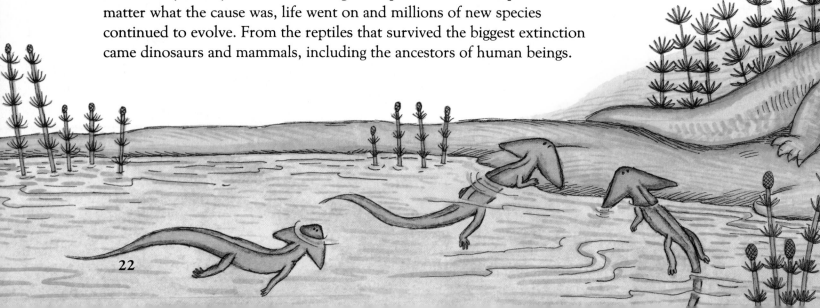

The Big Freeze

If you live in the northern United States, in Canada, in northern Europe, or northern Asia, there is a good chance that about 15,000 years ago your land was covered by a sheet of ice more than half a mile thick. Such an ice sheet is called a continental glacier. Glaciers form only in places where the climate is very cold. Otherwise, the ice would melt.

When a glacier moves (very slowly), tons of ice scrape and scour the ground. The ice rips out rocks of all sizes and carries them along. Grooves are gouged out of softer rocks. When a glacier reaches a place warm enough for it to melt, the rocks it carries are left behind in ridges and mounds. Scientists can tell how much land was covered by glaciers from scrapes, grooves, ridges, and other such clues.

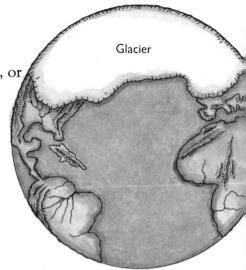

Glacier

Earth 15,000 years ago

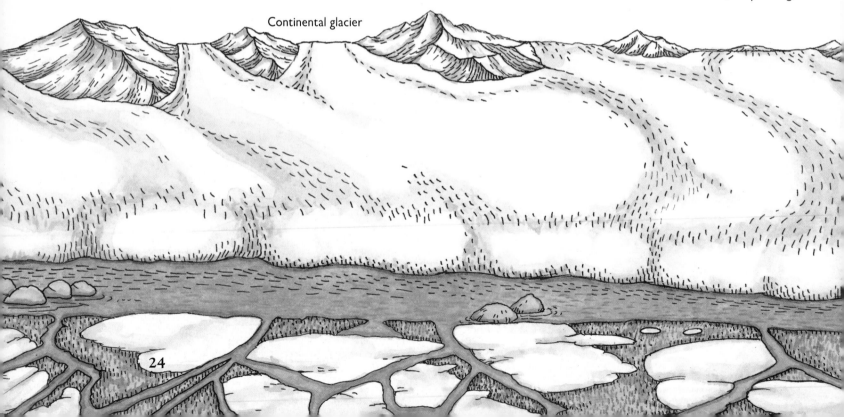

Continental glacier

24

Marks left by glaciers in rocks found today ew York City

Fifteen thousand years ago, Earth was in the grip of the great Ice Age. This time in Earth's history spanned more that one million years. At least four times in that million years the climate in many parts of the world turned cold enough for massive ice sheets to move down and cover the land. The movement of these ice sheets took place over a few hundred thousand years. Four times the climate eventually warmed and the ice melted until the cold returned again.

During the Ice Age, many living things became extinct. When the climate turned cold, animals that could survive only in warmer places had to move there or die. Plant species could not move on their own. If their seeds weren't carried to a place where the climate was warmer, the plants might become extinct.

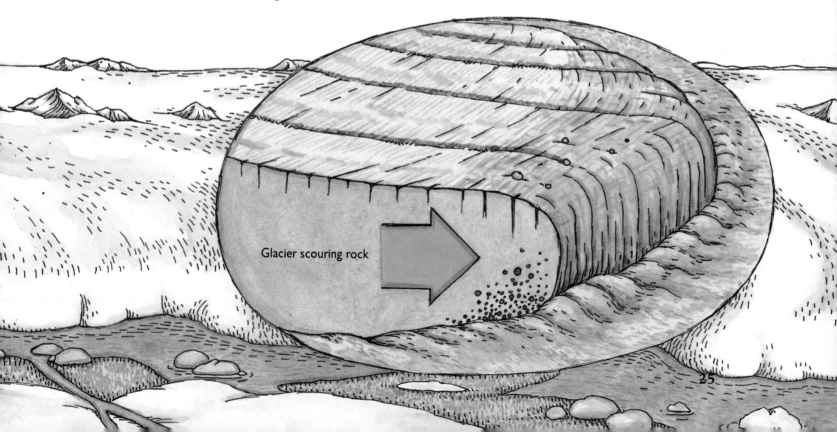

Glacier scouring rock

As the glaciers formed, they stored up more and more water as ice. The illustration shows that this water came from the oceans. The loss caused the oceans to pull away from the land. Many creatures that lived underwater along coasts could no longer survive in the open air. Then as the glaciers moved, the ice flattened forests, filled valleys, and blocked rivers. Species that lived in these areas were destroyed.

Yet Another Mystery

Fifteen thousand years does not sound all that long ago. Compared to one million years, it isn't. However, 15,000 years ago North America was home to mastodons and mammoths, horses, camels, and long-horned

Snow

Glacier

Evaporation

Land

Ocean

Water evaporates from the ocean, enters the air, forms clouds. Over land where the climate is very snow falls in winter but doesn't fully melt in summ Year after year the unmelted snow can turn into form glaciers. If the climate remains very cold, the glaciers get bigger and bigger, locking up more an water that came from the ocean. This causes the to shrink. Only when the climate warms and the melt does the water return to the oceans.

melting glacier

bisons. Saber-toothed cats sunk their long, curved, sharp teeth into giant ground sloths and hungry dire wolves stalked whatever prey they could find.

All of these large mammals and many others ceased to exist in North America by the time the last ice sheets melted about 10,000 years ago. They became extinct while most sea animals and smaller land animals did not. Like all good detectives, scientists have to look at every clue to solve a mystery. The remains of weapons found near bones of long-horned bison and other extinct animals suggest that humans hunted the creatures to extinction.

Is the great Ice Age over? Will the glaciers return in a few thousand years to cover New York City, Chicago, Montreal, and Vancouver? No one knows.

27

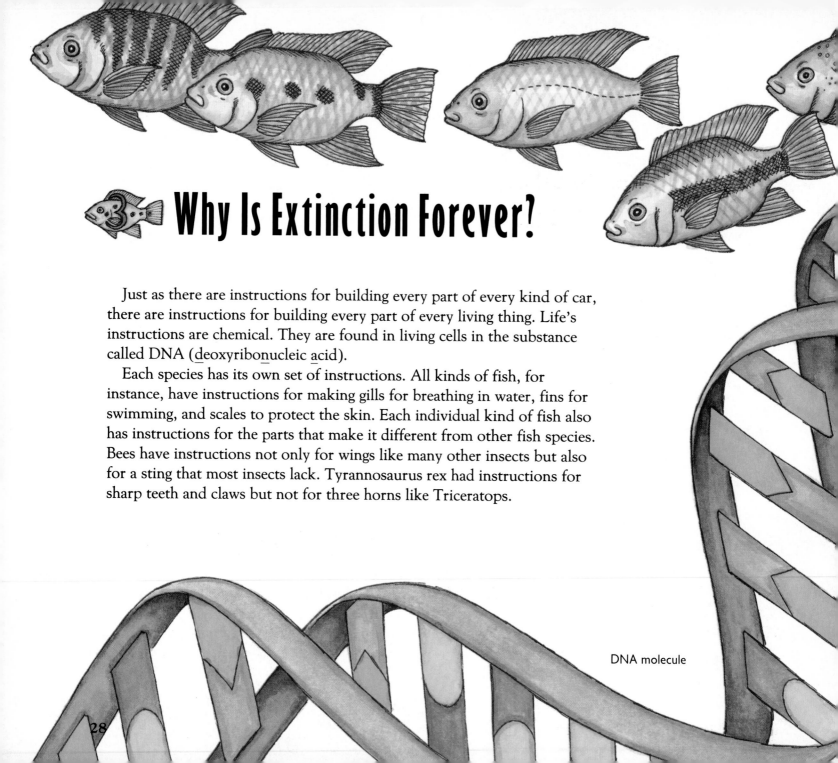

Why Is Extinction Forever?

Just as there are instructions for building every part of every kind of car, there are instructions for building every part of every living thing. Life's instructions are chemical. They are found in living cells in the substance called DNA (<u>d</u>eoxyribo<u>n</u>ucleic <u>a</u>cid).

Each species has its own set of instructions. All kinds of fish, for instance, have instructions for making gills for breathing in water, fins for swimming, and scales to protect the skin. Each individual kind of fish also has instructions for the parts that make it different from other fish species. Bees have instructions not only for wings like many other insects but also for a sting that most insects lack. Tyrannosaurus rex had instructions for sharp teeth and claws but not for three horns like Triceratops.

DNA molecule

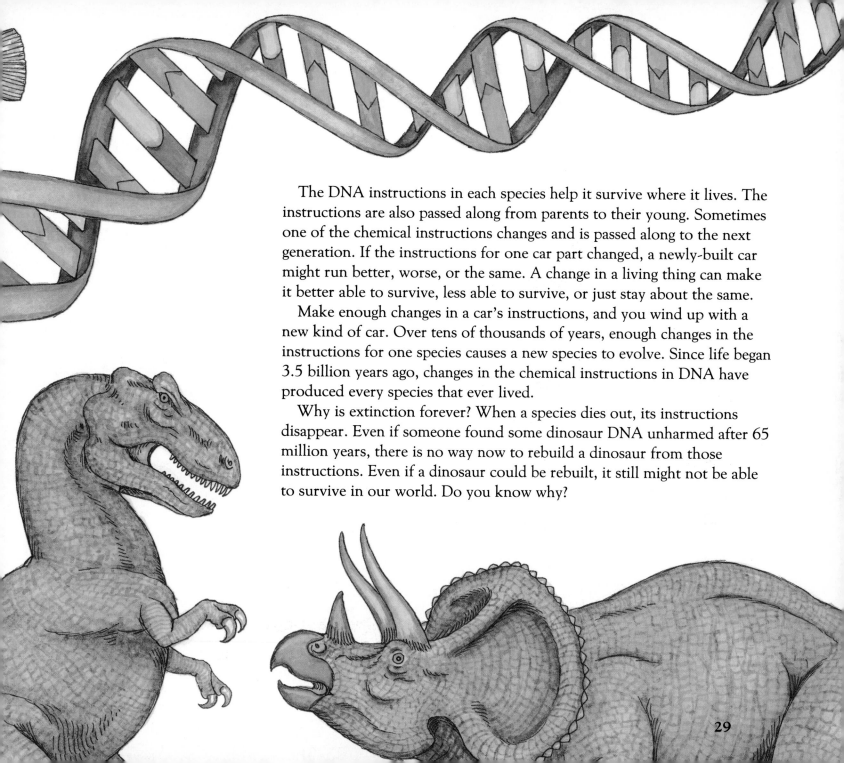

The DNA instructions in each species help it survive where it lives. The instructions are also passed along from parents to their young. Sometimes one of the chemical instructions changes and is passed along to the next generation. If the instructions for one car part changed, a newly-built car might run better, worse, or the same. A change in a living thing can make it better able to survive, less able to survive, or just stay about the same.

Make enough changes in a car's instructions, and you wind up with a new kind of car. Over tens of thousands of years, enough changes in the instructions for one species causes a new species to evolve. Since life began 3.5 billion years ago, changes in the chemical instructions in DNA have produced every species that ever lived.

Why is extinction forever? When a species dies out, its instructions disappear. Even if someone found some dinosaur DNA unharmed after 65 million years, there is no way now to rebuild a dinosaur from those instructions. Even if a dinosaur could be rebuilt, it still might not be able to survive in our world. Do you know why?

 # Good or Bad?

Imagine what the world would be like if nothing happened 65 million years ago and dinosaurs were still alive. Would there be room for humans? Would humans exist?

Human beings evolved from the small mammals that survived when the dinosaurs didn't. So did cats, dogs, rabbits, elephants, and all other mammals of today. If the dinosaurs kept on living, those small mammals might have become extinct sometime later.

By destroying species that have been on Earth for thousands or millions of years, extinction makes room for new species. Is the extinction process good for allowing this to happen? Or is extinction bad for not allowing all species that evolve to just keep on living? When extinction happens in nature, it isn't good or bad. It is part of the way nature works: *Living things evolve, and living things become extinct.*

Nature's Best Kept Secret

So far, even during the biggest extinction of all, some species were able to survive whatever killed off the rest. The species that stayed alive didn't know in advance that a mass extinction was about to happen. They survived because something about the way they lived kept them from being destroyed.

Nature's weapon to keep extinction from ending life on Earth is the diversity or variety of species. The more ways species have of finding food, escaping predators, building nests, spreading seeds, and adjusting to climate changes, the greater chance there is that during a mass extinction some kind of life will always survive.

Nature's best kept secret is how it keeps restocking Earth with a wide variety of living things after each extinction. New kinds of plants that make their own food evolve as do new kinds of animals that eat the plants. New kinds of predators appear that eat the plant eaters. Creatures that live in the soil, at the bottom of the ocean, in fields and forests, in deserts and caves also appear and evolve. Extinction may be forever, but so far life goes on.

5. What's Going On?

Save the pandas! Save the whales! Save the tigers! Save the condors!

What do all of these creatures have to be saved from? The answer is extinction. Is there a mass extinction going on right now? If so, what is causing it and why don't you know about it? Surely every newspaper, magazine, and television news show would be reporting the crash of an asteroid, exploding volcanoes, or a climate change. Yet around the world, many scientists, conservationists, and nature lovers are convinced this is a time of mass extinction. They believe the mass extinction is being caused by humans.

No one can tell when it began—maybe with the disappearance of the mammoths and other large mammals 10,000 years ago. Since then, life on Earth has changed as humans took over the planet.

Unlike fish, human beings can't breathe underwater. Humans don't grow wings like birds, bats, and butterflies. They aren't as strong as elephants or as fast as cheetahs. They don't see, hear, or smell as well as many animals; and they can't capture the sun's energy like plants. What humans can do is think, learn, speak, and invent. Using their brains, humans figured out how to grow their own food, control fire, use tools, read, write, cure diseases, build machines, probe the atom, even fly to the moon and back. In just a few thousand years, humans dominated land, sea, and sky. Or did they?

Something happened as more and more people filled this planet. Farmland replaced forest; and later towns, cities, and factories replaced many farms. Roads and railroad tracks reached everywhere that people lived and worked. The places where animals and plants lived became smaller and smaller.

People hunted whales to make oil for lamps; and hunted seals, leopards, and sables to make fur coats. The demand for ivory sent them after elephants; and the fashion craze for hat feathers cost many ostriches, egrets, and other birds their lives. To protect their crops from hungry insects, farmers sprayed poisons that soaked into the soil to be washed into rivers and streams.

People took whatever they wanted from the world around them as if the riches of the Earth would never run out. Humans did what they wanted to the land, water, and air never thinking the elements could be harmed. They made a serious mistake.

The Supply Can Run Out

No matter how long and hard you search, you won't be able to find a passenger pigeon living on Earth. With so many other kinds of pigeons around, that may not mean much. In the 1800s, however, people would have said it was impossible for passenger pigeons to vanish from North America.

Countless millions of passenger pigeons flew across the continent in huge flocks. So many would fly by at one time that they darkened the sky. Hunters found them easy targets and hungry families ate them. No one could see anything wrong in going out and shooting a passenger pigeon, or two, or three, or four....

Slowly at first the number of passenger pigeons declined. Then each year fewer and fewer flocks flew by. That also meant fewer and fewer eggs were laid and chicks raised. Still, not many people took notice. After all, there was no reason to worry because the pigeons would no doubt be back. Finally, a big reward was offered to anyone who found a nesting pair of passenger pigeons. No one claimed the money.

Passenger pigeons weren't the first birds to become extinct because of humans. Until about the year 1800 dodo birds lived on islands in the Indian Ocean. Dodos grew to be about the size of turkeys, could not fly, and were found nowhere else on Earth. When explorers and settlers came to the islands, they began to catch dodos to eat. This did not wipe out all the dodos. The settlers also brought pigs and dogs to the islands. These animals destroyed the dodos' nests and ate their young.

Perhaps if the settlers had known that there were no dodos anywhere else, they might have protected the birds from extinction. Indeed, moas, quaggas, Steller's sea cows, great auks, and so many other species that are gone forever might have been saved if people learned sooner that "the supply can run out."

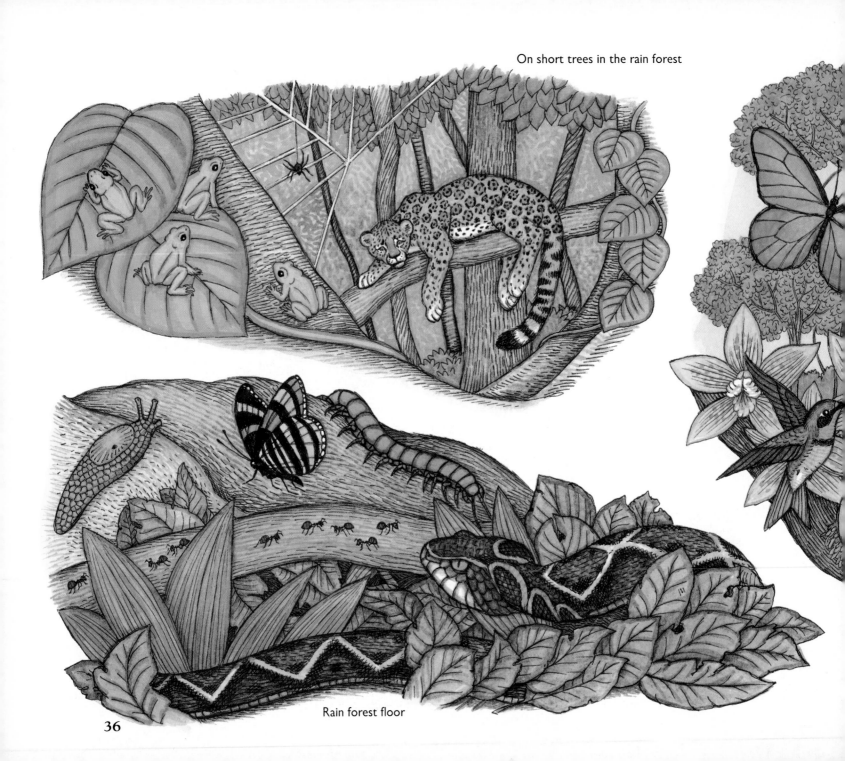

On short trees in the rain forest

Rain forest floor

Rain forest canopy

No Place Like Home

From mountains to prairies, from deserts to seashores, in river valleys and on islands, humans can and do live just about everywhere. The story is different for plants and animals. Each species has a natural home called a *habitat* where it is best able to survive. A bullfrog, for instance, lives in a pond. It would die in a desert. A zebra needs a lot more space than a bullfrog. Its grassland habitat spreads over hundreds of miles.

More kinds of plants and animals live in one habitat than in any other. That habitat is the tropical rain forest located near the equator. Like other habitats, the tropical rain forest supplies the needs of the plants and animals that live in it. Each rain forest species does its share to make the habitat work for all the species. Plants, for example, make food. Insects, birds, and bats help plants reproduce by carrying pollen from one plant to another. Creatures in the soil help recycle wastes and decompose dead plant and animal bodies. All the species depend on each other to keep the rain forest alive.

Life fills every nook and cranny of the tropical rain forest from the ground to the tops of the tallest trees. Army ants march along the forest floor. Slugs and centipedes hide from the ants, and snakes lie in wait for their next meal to appear. Above, on short trees, spiders spin webs, a jaguar sleeps, and poisonous frogs show off their bright colors as a warning to predators to stay away. Higher up in the canopy where trees open like umbrellas, orchids and ferns grow along tree branches as if they were soil. Colorful birds, butterflies, and beetles move in among the leaves hardly disturbing sleeping bats or monkeys at play. Above the canopy in the tallest trees, eagles and hawks peer below for a monkey or snake to seize.

Tropical rain forests are so alive that no one yet knows how many species live in them. There may be millions—between 50 and 90 percent of all species alive on Earth. Most of the species haven't been named or even discovered.

Disappearing Habitats

Most tropical rain forests are in countries where too many of the people are poor and landless. To improve their lives and to build a better future for their children, some of these people have been cutting down rain forests and turning them into farms for growing crops and ranches for raising cattle. A piece of rain forest the size of a football field is cut down every second of every day. If this destruction doesn't stop, all of Earth's tropical rain forests will disappear in less than 100 years.

In the meantime, plant and animal species are becoming extinct. Many live in just one part of one rain forest. When that part is gone, so are they—forever. Other species die out when the food they eat is destroyed. Twenty or more animal species, for example, may depend on one kind of plant for food. If that plant becomes extinct, they will become extinct too. The animals that eat them may have a harder time staying alive. If the rain forests completely disappear, so will more than half of all the world's species.

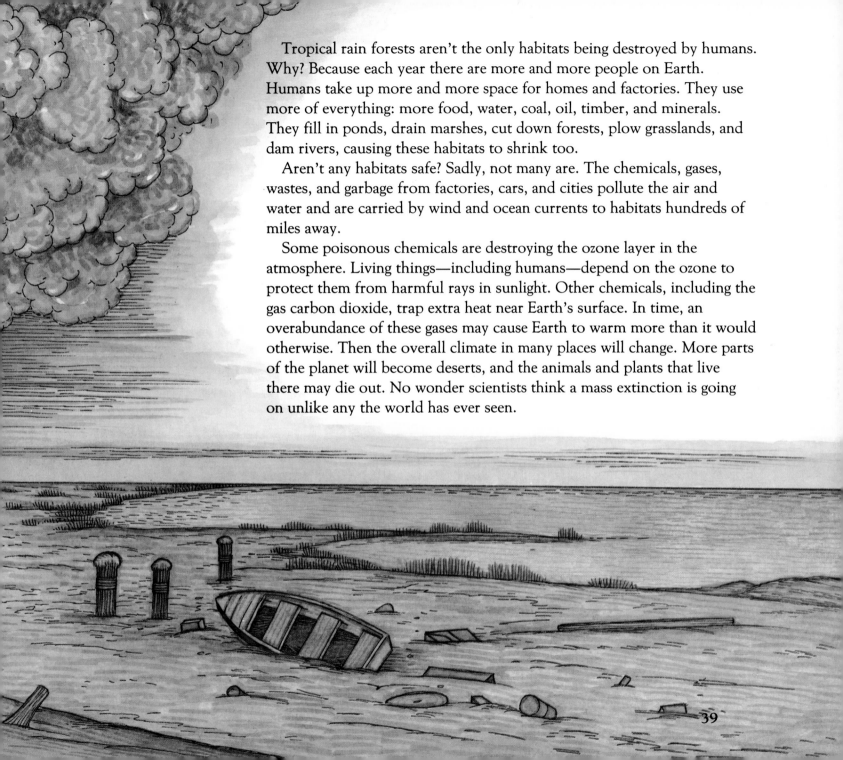

Tropical rain forests aren't the only habitats being destroyed by humans. Why? Because each year there are more and more people on Earth. Humans take up more and more space for homes and factories. They use more of everything: more food, water, coal, oil, timber, and minerals. They fill in ponds, drain marshes, cut down forests, plow grasslands, and dam rivers, causing these habitats to shrink too.

Aren't any habitats safe? Sadly, not many are. The chemicals, gases, wastes, and garbage from factories, cars, and cities pollute the air and water and are carried by wind and ocean currents to habitats hundreds of miles away.

Some poisonous chemicals are destroying the ozone layer in the atmosphere. Living things—including humans—depend on the ozone to protect them from harmful rays in sunlight. Other chemicals, including the gas carbon dioxide, trap extra heat near Earth's surface. In time, an overabundance of these gases may cause Earth to warm more than it would otherwise. Then the overall climate in many places will change. More parts of the planet will become deserts, and the animals and plants that live there may die out. No wonder scientists think a mass extinction is going on unlike any the world has ever seen.

In Need of Help

During the 1950s and 1960s, farmers sprayed the chemical DDT to kill the insects eating their crops. DDT did its job well, but it also soaked into the soil and washed into rivers and streams. In the water, plants and tiny animals absorbed small amounts of DDT. That DDT was passed along to little fish that ate the plants and animals. When big fish ate lots of little fish, DDT built up inside their bodies. And when bald eagles ate big fish, DDT became stored inside the eagles.

It took awhile before people noticed that there weren't as many bald eagles as there used to be. The DDT wasn't killing the eagles. Instead, the chemical harmed their eggs so that fewer and fewer chicks were hatching. By the time DDT was banned in 1970, the bald eagle had become an *endangered* species.

An endangered species is one at great risk of becoming extinct if nothing is done to save it. Banning DDT in the 1970s did help because the number of eagle chicks has increased since then. However, more than 1,000 other endangered species are now known. There may be millions more such as those in the rain forests that don't even have a name.

Finding and identifying endangered species isn't enough. By the time a species is endangered, it may be too late to save it from extinction. Once too few of a species exist to have healthy young, soon none will be left. That's why it is important to pinpoint species at risk of becoming endangered.

Even that isn't enough. What good is saving a species if it has nowhere to live, to find food, or to raise its young? Habitats must be saved because only in a species' natural home will it best be able to survive and reproduce.

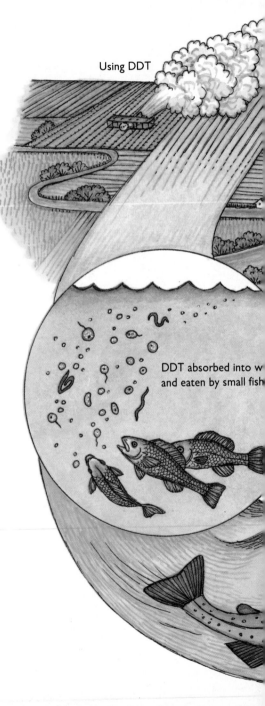

Using DDT

DDT absorbed into w
and eaten by small fish

Eagles eat big fish

Big fish eat small fish

Eagle eggs don't hatch

41

Extinction Is Forever

Extinction *is* forever but the extinction humans cause is not the same as nature's extinctions. Whenever there has been a mass extinction in nature, the variety of life always bounced back, even if it took millions of years. The species that survived were the ones selected by nature. Humans do not know why or how only those species were able to keep on living, but they did.

When humans cause extinction, they bypass nature. Nature doesn't get the chance to work the way it should. Species are lost, and quickly. Species are disappearing before humans even learn how much nature needs them. This is harmful because humans also depend on nature for soil, water, air, minerals, climate, energy, and for everything else that makes life on Earth possible. If so many species become extinct that nature stops working the way it should, humans may find themselves in danger. There is no reason for that to happen, because humans have the ability to make decisions and take action.

Humans can stop cutting down the rain forests. They can set aside habitats as wildlife preserves. Like the Hawaiian islanders who are trying to keep out the brown tree snake, people living in other parts of the world can be on the watch for species invading habitats where they do not belong. Humans also have to change the ways they live. They have to learn to care about all living things, not just the plants and animals they eat or their pets. Once people stop wanting so much, wasting so much, and polluting so much, habitats will be saved and extinction will be controlled by nature, not by humans.

You Can Help

There are steps you can take to help save wildlife and habitats. Reuse and recycle paper and plastics. Save energy by turning off electric lights when they are not needed. Take care of habitats near where you live and wherever you visit by not littering and by never harming a living thing. Ask your family not to buy rain forest birds or any other animals as pets that were taken from the wild. Don't buy fur coats or any other clothing that is made of a wild animal.

The more you learn about the way nature works, the more you will understand why people should stop causing species to vanish. One day you may even help solve the mystery of what really happened to the dinosaurs.

All About Fossils

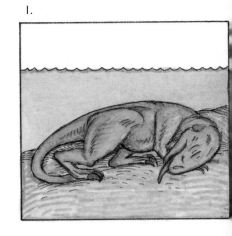

Fossils are clues to unlocking the mysteries of Earth's past. They help scientists piece together the history of life on Earth. They reveal only part of the story, however. When most living things died, they were eaten or they rotted away without leaving anything behind. Then how did dinosaur and other fossils form?

Sometimes a dinosaur died in a swamp or lake or fell into the water. (1) There the dinosaur was quickly covered with a layer of mud or sand. Soft body parts such as skin kept decaying and disappeared. Bones and teeth remained. (2)

Over thousands of years, layer upon layer of ooze covered the bones and teeth. The upper layers pressed down and squeezed the lower layers together until they formed rock. During this time, minerals in the water filled any space in the bones and teeth. When the minerals hardened, the bones and teeth became fossils made of stone. (3)

Over thousands of more years, the swamps and lakes dried up. Later the ocean flooded the land and more layers of rock formed. When the ocean withdrew, the rocks with the fossils inside lay hidden underground. They may still be hidden unless earthquakes, rising mountains, or canyons cutting through the Earth bring the rocks near the surface. (4)

Not all fossils are bones and teeth that turned to stone. In some places, for instance, a bone dissolved leaving only its impression in rock. That imprint is still a fossil. The outline of a leaf or of a feather pressed into rock is also a fossil. Footprints of dinosaurs made in soft mud turned into fossils when the mud hardened into rock. The skeleton of a saber-toothed

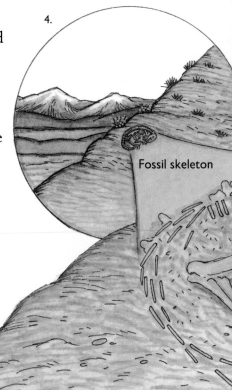

Fossil skeleton

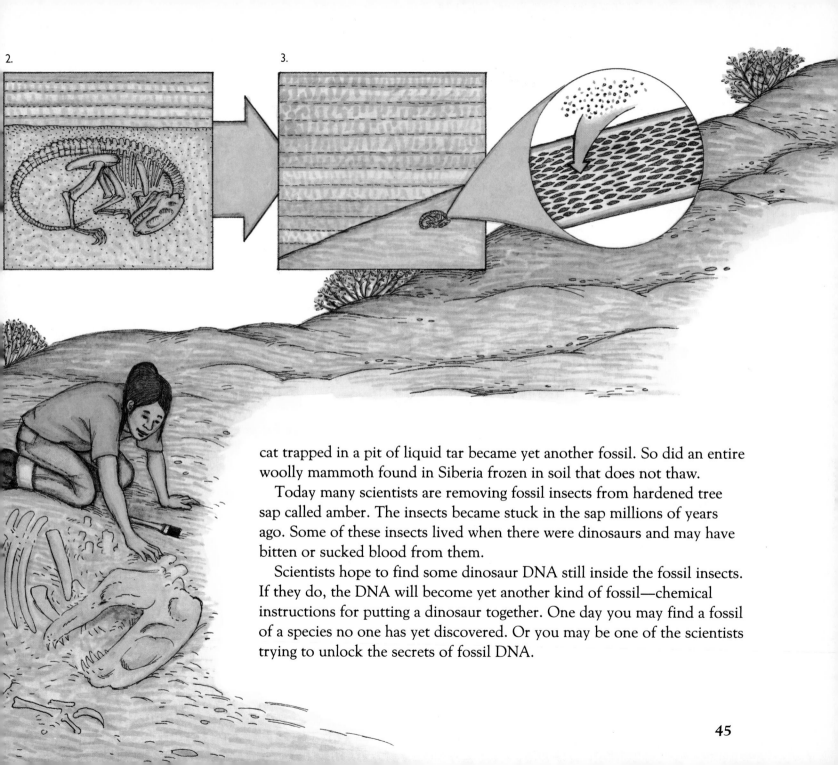

2.

3.

cat trapped in a pit of liquid tar became yet another fossil. So did an entire woolly mammoth found in Siberia frozen in soil that does not thaw.

Today many scientists are removing fossil insects from hardened tree sap called amber. The insects became stuck in the sap millions of years ago. Some of these insects lived when there were dinosaurs and may have bitten or sucked blood from them.

Scientists hope to find some dinosaur DNA still inside the fossil insects. If they do, the DNA will become yet another kind of fossil—chemical instructions for putting a dinosaur together. One day you may find a fossil of a species no one has yet discovered. Or you may be one of the scientists trying to unlock the secrets of fossil DNA.

Further Reading

Aliki. *Digging Up Dinosaurs*. New York: Thomas Y. Crowell, 1981.

———. *Fossils Tell of Long Ago*. New York: Thomas Y. Crowell, 1990.

Bramley, Franklyn M. *What Happened to the Dinosaurs?* New York: Thomas Y. Crowell, 1989.

Eldredge, Niles, Gregory Eldredge, and Douglas Eldredge. *The Fossil Factory*. Reading: MA: Addison Wesley, 1989.

Lauber, Patricia. *Dinosaurs Walked Here and Other Stories Fossils Tell*. New York: Bradbury Press, 1987.

Lindsey, William. *The Great Dinosaur Atlas*. New York: Julian Messner, 1991.

McGowan, Chris. *Discover Dinosaurs*. Reading, MA: Addison Wesley, 1989.

Silver, Donald. *Why Save the Rain Forest?* New York: Julian Messner, 1993.

Wexo, John Bonnett. *Endangered Animals Zoobooks*. San Diego, CA: Wildlife Education Limited, 1983.

World Book. *Dinosaurs: A Supplement to Childcraft—The How and Why Library*. Chicago: World Book, 1987.

Flightless Caracara, extinct 1900

Quagga, extinct 1883

Texas Red Wolf, extinct 1970

West Indian Monk Seal, extinct 1954

Museums with Fossil Collections

Steller's Sea Cow,
extinct 1741

Pink-Headed Duck,
extinct 1935

To find out more about extinction and fossils,
visit or write to the following museums.
They all have excellent fossil collections.

American Museum of Natural History, New York, NY

Buffalo Museum of Science, Buffalo, NY

Carnegie Museum of Natural History, Pittsburg, PA

Cleveland Museum of Natural History, Cleveland, OH

Denver Museum of Natural History, Denver, CO

Dinosaur National Monument, Jensen, UT

Field Museum of Natural History, Chicago, IL

Fort Worth Museum of Science, Fort Worth, TX

Los Angeles County Museum of Natural History, Los Angeles, CA

Museum of Comparative Zoology, Cambridge, MA

Museum of Northern Arizona, Flagstaff, AZ

Museum of Natural History, Princeton, NJ

National Museum of Natural History, Washington, DC

Peabody Museum of Natural History, New Haven, CT

University of Michigan Exhibit Museum, Ann Arbor, MI

University Natural History Museum, Boulder, CO

University of Wyoming Geological Museum, Laramie, WY

Utah Museum of Natural History, Salt Lake City, UT

National Museum of Natural Science, Ottawa, Ontario, Canada

Provincial Museum of Alberta, Edmonton, Alberta, Canada

Redpath Museum, McGill University, Montreal, Quebec, Canada

Royal Ontario Museum, Toronto, Ontario, Canada

Tryell Museum of Paleontology, Drumheller, Alberta, Canada

Zoological Gardens, Calgary, Alberta, Canada

British Museum of Natural History, London, England

Sedgwick Museum, Cambridge, England

University Museum, Oxford, England

National Museum of Natural History, Paris, France

National Science Museum, Tokyo, Japan

Hare-Lipped Suckerfish, extinct 1893

Index

Bold numbers indicate illustrations.